371·3

Creating Positive Cl

Other Classmates:

2nd Series
Successful Subject Co-ordination – Christine Farmery
Parent Partnership in the Early Years – Damien Fitzgerald
Playing Outdoors in the Early Years – Ros Garrick
Assemblies Made Easy – Victoria Kidwell
Homework – Victoria Kidwell
Getting Promoted – Tom Miller
ICT in the Early Years – Mark O'Hara
Getting Organized – Angela Thody and Derek Bowden
Physical Development in the Early Years – Lynda Woodfield

1st Series
Lesson Planning – Graham Butt
Managing Your Classroom – Gererd Dixie
Teacher's Guide to Protecting Children – Janet Kay
Tips for Trips – Andy Leeder
Stress Busting – Michael Papworth
Every Minute Counts – Michael Papworth
Teaching Poetry – Fred Sedgwick
Running Your Tutor Group – Ian Startup
Involving Parents – Julian Stern
Marking and Assessment – Howard Tanner

Creating Positive Classrooms

Mike Ollerton

continuum
LONDON • NEW YORK

Continuum
The Tower Building
11 York Road
London SE1 7NX

15 East 26th Street
New York
NY 10010

www.continuumbooks.com

British Library Cataloguing-in-Publication Data
A catalogue record for this book is available from the British Library.

ISBN: 0–8264–7310–5 (paperback)

Typeset by BookEns Ltd, Royston, Herts.
Printed and bound in Great Britain by
Antony Rowe Ltd, Chippenham, Wiltshire

Contents

Contents

*All royalties from this book will be paid to
Save the Children*

Acknowledgements

My great thanks go to Anne, Brenda, James and Mike for giving me permission to interview them about the values they take into their classrooms and schools and to glimpse aspects of their practice. Yet again I thank Alexandra Webster for having the confidence in my capability to write this book and for encouraging me to complete it without having to desert my beloved Lakeland fells too frequently! Anne's phrase *gentling the profession* is one that will stay with me and, I intend, shall positively influence my values as a teacher.

Introduction

Life at the chalk face is complex. This is because every teacher has to find ways of working with children who are different from each other, who have different needs, different motivations, different amounts of support at home, and different aspirations. The plethora of situations that occur in a classroom must be weighed up and often quickly responded to; at the same time teachers seek to interact with students in ways that, as far as is possible, are seen to be 'fair'. How a teacher responds to a similar situation that occurs in a classroom is based upon a) their perception of different students' needs, and b) the most effective way of interacting with different individuals. Responses and interactions are determined by values that guide a teacher's practice; this is all part of the complexity of being a teacher. It is the importance of developing sound working relationships with students and having to deal with complexity that makes teaching such an exhausting yet a brilliant job.

This book, therefore, is about school ethos and classroom culture and is based upon the notion that schools do not exist within a black or white world, nor do they operate from a perspective of a perfect or a Utopian world. Individual teachers though do aspire towards constructing a version of Utopia in their classrooms and, in support of this, school managers have significant responsibilities to carry out. Such responsibilities are discharged through the role models they present, the whole-school policies they help formulate and through styles of management. What is paramount is that teachers feel they are supported and valued when dealing with a highly complex range of issues and situations.

Given the multi-faceted nature of teaching, teachers certainly have to find ways of dealing with the range of situations that arise, some of which are predictable and others wholly unpredictable. However, if we assume from the outset that not every student in a class is necessarily going to adhere to the instructions we give, hear what we say, or even be interested in what we have to offer, a different complexion on how we might respond to such eventualities arises.

How teachers manage their classrooms and achieve control and discipline is complex; this is the case whether a teacher is charming and charismatic or the most hardened disciplinarian. These ways of characterizing forms of teacher behaviour exist at either end of a spectrum, for most of us mere mortals we have to work in between such extremes; using a range of ways of responding to events and vacillating on a continuum between such extremes. There are no quick answers and no easy solutions. Teaching cannot be objectified to the point of action and reaction, 'crime' and punishment, achievement and reward; life is not so simple. The more we engage with the complexity of teaching and search out ways of responding to events, so students feel cared for as individuals, then the more we are capable of creating positive relationships. The more positive relationships we create with students then the less likely or the less frequently the need for making use of sanctions such as, for example, a detention system.

This book is set out in two main sections. The first considers wider issues of teacher development and teachers' values. To explore the latter I include extracts from interviews with four teachers who were prepared to be interviewed to discuss their 'values in action'. In the second part of the book I explore more specific issues that impact upon the life of every school. These issues are about detention, the giving (or not) of prizes, and smoking. For example, I consider how certain 'givens', such as a percentage of children who smoke impacts upon the way schools and individual teachers are expected to respond by wider society. I balance this against what the reality is for individual teachers who have to take on the tobacco industry! I also consider the possible impacts that issues relating to smoking detention systems and merit marks have upon students and the school ethos.

Throughout I consider how these issues and teachers' responses to them underpin the different ways students experience school.

The ethos of a school and the culture of teachers' classrooms

There exists a whole multitude of factors, external to schools, which schools can do little or nothing

Introduction

about. At best a school can attempt to compensate for or offer its students different perspectives; creating the possibility of alternative ways that students might respond to the influences upon their lives. For example, a couple of years ago I was driving up the M6 to a school to work with and observe a trainee teacher. It was 8.10 am and for some reason I began to 'surf' the radio channels. My attention was caught by a young DJ who began to make all kinds of 'male', over-the top (in a mildly sexual and highly personal manner), subjective and assertive type of comments. Even worse, there appeared to be two or three other background 'commentators' who were laughing about, egging on and encouraging the lead DJ to continue to make banal and inflammatory statements. With the cajoling in the background, the whole vein became nonsensical; it wasn't even funny. It was almost as if these people had taken the responsibility to fill the local radio airwaves with arbitrary, trite, childish and opinionated statements which, in the heads of some adolescents', could be highly anti-social and at worst dangerous. The comments and the nature by which they were transmitted were completely lacking in any sense of humility or care for what they were saying or what messages they were sending out.

Despite the outpouring, I was transfixed by just how much worse the banter and the background noise was becoming. Whilst I was subjected to this banality I thought about how many of the students in the schools in the city would also be listening. Then it occurred to me that students across the country would be getting themselves filled up with this kind of hype and their teachers would somehow have to find ways of de-hyping them, of combating the education students were gaining through their radios; teachers would have to try to offer students different ways of being, of talking, of sharing, of caring and of learning. My next thought concerned the responsibility that schools and teachers are expected to take on board, in terms of educating the youth and how there are so many outside influences that militate against the roles teachers are expected to and have to play.

Schools, therefore, have a lot to contend with and as such the ethos a school creates is vital to the way its students might see what alternatives there are for developing other, perhaps gentler, less aggress-ive, less immediately selfish ways of being and thinking. Coming to understand that the strongest, the fastest or the loudest are not necessarily the 'bestest' is not an easy job, especially when the strongest, the fastest and the loudest are often given the greatest credence; popularity all too readily displaces quality.

Helping students achieve their potential and develop their talents is a significant challenge for schools and teachers; as such, much depends upon the ethos a school has, the implicit messages a school transmits and the models that individual teachers offer.

Ethos and culture can only be created by staff and students and actively put into practice during all types of interactions throughout the school day, not only in classrooms but in assemblies, in dining halls,

Introduction

in corridors and on school trips. Other ways a school attempts to place students at the centre of its activity might be through a school council and the powers regarding decision-making such a body is conferred with. I have heard of one school that sets up an interview panel made up of students who conduct one of the interviews for prospective members of staff and give feedback to the headteacher. Ceding such responsibility to students, so they can voice an opinion, is significant in terms of positively encouraging part ownership of decision-making processes within their school. Another context where the ethos of a school is enacted might, for example, be in a dining hall. Creating a pleasant atmosphere in the school dining room is strongly dependent upon the nature of the relationships that exist between kitchen staff, other adults and students, as well as the quality of food on offer and the expectations of what a canteen is for.

The underlying issue here is about the value of social interactions that occur in a school. Such considerations may seem something of a departure from a specific issue, such as awarding merit marks. Yet if merit marks are awarded, then this is also part of the ethos of the school and someone must have made an active decision to implement such a system. When the ethos of a school promotes healthy, positive interactions between adults and students, then students, in turn, develop positive attitudes based upon the pleasure of being in a place for what it has to offer than, necessarily, for any extrinsic rewards that may be on offer.

It is always interesting to walk into a school and feel its 'vibes', to gain a sense of what kind of a place the school is. Trying to define what it is that creates a pleasant atmosphere is a little bit like squeezing jelly. There are so many variables, symbols and attributes to take into account that it becomes impossible to say whether one approach to education is better than another approach. Whether a school has a uniform or not is a good example. Having worked for many years in a school which did not have any uniform, I can vouch that this school was no less orderly by comparison to the dozens of other schools I have visited all of which have a uniform of one sort or another. To suppose that a uniform creates a sense of order might suggest that those schools which do not have a uniform are therefore disorderly. However, this is not the case; what creates 'order' and a positive ethos in a school are the relationships that exist between teachers and students; the ways teachers and students respond and talk to each other are crucial to the well-being of a school. The nature of the display work that adorns walls and the photographs of events are all important ways that a school presents itself. Even whether the head-teacher chooses to exercise her/his status by having a marked car-parking space (usually the closest one to the school entrance) presents a visitor with a symbol about what the head of a school sees, or wishes others to see, as being of importance.

Schools face huge challenges to encourage students to make sense of what they are taught and at the same time learn the value of compassion, humility and the importance of self-improvement. On top of this, there is the incredible rate of physical and mental changes that students go through. This book is an attempt to provide a contribution to help teachers to achieve such aims and to engage with some of the challenges.

To conclude this introduction I offer the following thought about the numerous stakeholders who invest different amounts of time and energy in influencing how we teach. In order of priority I list them as follows: students, parents/guardians, colleagues, school managers, governors, government and their quangos (including inspectors) and the media. The impact these people/organizations have or would like to have upon how schools and teachers operate in order of importance might well be read in reverse!

All governments want to raise standards in education yet, because they also want to be re-elected, governments need to ensure the policies they design and fund are seen to be effective; and such information and measures of success are transmitted through the media. In order, for policies to be seen to be working, simple-to-understand information must be readily available. So, for example, measures of success are frequently quoted as the percentage of A to C grades individual schools gain at GCSE or the number of level 4s, 5s and so on, that primary school children gain from national tests.

However, the measures of 'failure' are far more complex to determine. Obviously, it is not feasible to have success without also having failure. In my opinion it is this false construction and measurement of success that also creates failure. Rarely do we hear of those who gain D to G grades at GCSE being considered as successes, this despite the fact that for some students who gain a grade G, such an achievement will be a considerable success ... life at the chalk face is indeed complex.

Part One: Positive Thinking

1

Teacher Development

> *Adding wings to caterpillars does not create butterflies – it creates awkward and dysfunctional caterpillars. Butterflies are created through transformation.*
>
> Stephanie Pace Marshall (quoted in Davies and Edwards 1999)

A student recently asked me: *'What makes a good teacher?'* In those milliseconds when we know a response is expected of us, a multitude of thoughts passed between my wires such as: *'This is a "big" question'*, *'How do I begin to answer this one'*, and, *'What does "good" mean anyway?'*. I offered a response: *'A good learner'*, and we continued our conversation. One aspect of being a 'good' learner is to make sense of events, to see connections between what we know and new experiences that occur. One aspect, therefore, of teacher development is 'getting better' at what we do. To develop practice we need to know what it looks like in the first instance.

This chapter is about looking for ways of getting better at what we do, at transforming practice from what it looks like to what we want it to look like. The Stephanie Pace Marshall quote used in an article by Davies and Edwards offers an interesting perspective; particularly in the current climate of prescribed curriculum and described teaching methodologies it is important to consider what we can do for ourselves as teachers in terms of professional development. A potent form of development is something we *can* do ourselves and share with colleagues; this is reflecting upon, analysing and discussing practice.

Analysing our practice

How we walk, talk, smile, etc. identifies us as people. Others notice such characteristics in the way they see us and sometimes define us. A teacher's aura has a significant impact upon classroom culture; this is inescapable. What is important is the kind of culture we wish to create. How we go about working towards creating a classroom culture that supports effective learning, thus underpinning the way students respond to our teaching, is a crucial aspect of teacher development.

Knowing for ourselves what we do well and what areas of practice may require attention, are aspects of professional development that we can choose to work on. There are dangers of being overly critical, of focussing too much on what we don't do so well, and this can create a deficit model. More positively, becoming explicit about what we do well and knowing what our strengths are means gaining the confidence to open our practice up to scrutiny, to embrace perspectives from other professionals who enter our classroom without fear of criticism. At worst, inspection can result in a stranger entering our classroom and telling us of our weaknesses ... even being described as 'satisfactory' is a gauling prospect!

Knowing what we are successful at, however, is a positive place to begin and can lead us more cautiously into taking on board new initiatives, alternative practices, different ways of thinking, and considering other peoples' ideas and aims. The most important aspect in any teacher's development is how it impacts upon learning; the following quote from Sotto (1994:29) comes to mind: '... *it makes no sense to decide how one is going to teach, before one has made some study of how people learn.*'

To find out about our practice, what it looks, sounds and feels like with regard to how students learn is crucial; there are two main aspects to consider when exploring practice:

1. The classroom atmosphere.
2. The nature of interactions we have with students.

The second is clearly a subset of the first, however, because the moment-by-moment interactions we have with students are such an important part of learning and teaching. I will deal with these issues separately.

Exploring our practice – the classroom atmosphere and interacting with students

The atmosphere within which learning takes place is crucially important. Everyone is affected to some

Creating Positive Classrooms

extent by the context in which they work. In order to study how people learn, I must consider the kind of learning atmospheres I wish to create. Yet 'atmosphere' is a nebulous concept; to define classroom atmosphere it is useful to decide what makes an atmosphere and how anyone might perceive it. One way to define classroom atmosphere is to consider the following scenario.

Imagine a person you care a great deal about and consider this person briefly and unexpectedly entering your classroom. The person may have been standing at the open door for a couple of minutes, waiting for an appropriate moment before disturbing you. They might have an urgent message that they need to deliver in person, or they may want to give you a bunch of flowers – oh well, we can all live in hope!

Whatever the reason might be, some important questions are:

♦ What would you want this person to see, hear and feel about your classroom?

♦ What images would you want them to gain about you as a teacher?

Seeking answers to these questions as realistically as possible is one way of trying to determine what classroom atmosphere is and the kind of atmosphere we wish to create. Here are some examples of the type of thing we might wish our visitor to observe:

♦ Lots of work on the walls.

♦ See us talking with some students.

- Some students might be giving a presentation to the rest of the class about some work they have been doing.

- We might not be in the classroom though none of the students are taking advantage of our temporary absence.

Each image has implications for practice in terms of what we want the atmosphere of our classroom to be. How we purposefully achieve such outcomes, for they are not usually arrived at through good luck, is the central issue.

Constructing a positive, work-like, give-and-take classroom atmosphere demands a great deal of hard work; to know what kind of atmosphere we want it is necessary to know how we intend to achieve it. So if we believe that having lots of students' work on the wall is important then we need to find ways of making this happen, without it necessarily taking an inordinate amount of time.

A simple way of making the classroom look brighter can be achieved with posters. Posters for display can be made from anything that any student has learnt, whatever the magnitude of this learning or the task they have carried out might be. For example, if a student has finished reading a book, they could write/type out a review of the book. A print out could be enlarged using a large font; it then only requires a piece of sugar paper and a glue stick to turn this review into a poster. This has implications for the availability of such resources. Another student might, for the first time, understand how to multiply two decimal values together and again here the student can explain how they performed this task on a poster. We can analyse any area of the curriculum, extract the smallest piece of content knowledge and there exists the potential to turn any student's achievement into a poster.

This is similarly true for students giving presentations; encouraging an atmosphere where students are able to explain something they have just worked out or recently understood to the rest of the class is a more immediate, unplanned form of presentation. Planned presentations may require students, working in a pair or a group of three, to prepare overhead transparencies or use Powerpoint to disseminate what they have learnt over the course of a module.

The implication of students giving presentations is that we need to devote energy to encourage students to speak publicly to their peers. It is equally important for students to learn how to listen. However, this takes time and energy to achieve. If we feel this is a necessary part of the classroom atmosphere and an important aspect of students' social development, then we will find ways of making this happen in the classroom.

Posters and presentations are only two aspects of classroom atmosphere. Others include:

♦ how we want students to work;

♦ what kind of noise levels are acceptable and useful;

♦ whether to encourage students to decide for themselves who they wish to work with or whether we make such decisions for them.

Whatever we decide, it is necessary to be clear why we want such outcomes to occur, how we intend to achieve them and what our tolerance levels are.

Being a fly on the wall is a marvellous experience, particularly in terms of seeing what happens in other people's classrooms; it is also a privileged position to be in. How to create opportunities to become a fly on our own classroom wall is difficult though not impossible to achieve; developing self-awareness by analysing our actions and observing what is going on in our classroom, as it happens, is crucial to the process of personal development. Most of the time we operate on auto-pilot; this is not to suggest a style of teaching that is unthinking or uncaring but that our responses to certain situations and regularly occurring type of events are determined by instinct and experience.

To create spaces when we can more frequently become aware of events, I offer a strategy based upon basketball terminology of *taking a time-out*. As a fly on another person's classroom wall, to develop this issue of taking a time-out, I offer the following anecdote:

> I was observing a trainee teacher in a department where departing too far from a particular scheme was considered radical and, given the nature of the class being taught, encouraging students to work in groups, suicidal! The trainee was taking both of these issues on and although I believed him to be a competent trainee, there was a particular moment when I feared for the safe deliverance of the lesson.

He had explained to the class (a 'bottom' set Y10) they would be working on a problem and said he would be happy for them to work together, to share ideas and information. At this point one student asked if they could turn their desks around so they could work together in groups. Whilst I held my breath, the trainee held his nerve and agreed this would be OK. Thereupon desks and chairs were moved and I wondered how things were going to develop. Marvellously nothing did; within a minute the scraping of desk and chair legs on the bare wooden floor ceased and calmness pervaded. The trainee continued to have positive discussions with groups of students and so the lesson continued.

At the end when I asked him what he thought about the lesson and his reply demonstrated he had not fully appreciated what he had achieved. It seemed one reason for this was because he had been so busy engaging with students he had not had time to survey the classroom in order to see for himself what a splendid lesson he had been responsible for teaching. For him to be able to know what a 'good' lesson it was, to see for himself what the elements were that led to this being such a successful lesson, he would have needed to have been a fly on his own wall; by taking a time-out. By creating a personal time-out he might have stopped interacting and for a few moments stood at the back of the room, to see for himself the excellent working atmosphere he had created and how well the lesson was proceeding. This, I felt, was particularly the case because the Y10 students were textbook dependent, they were not used to problem solving-type lessons nor were they usually actively encouraged to talk to each other.

Meta-cognition is chiefly concerned with finding ways of being aware of one's actions and responses. Of course we cannot engage in meta-cognition all the time as teachers, otherwise it would be impossible to work on auto-pilot; as such we may do a lot of thinking about action but never get around to taking any! Meta-cognition, therefore, is an approach in teaching to help us decide what action might be most appropriate at certain times. In other words it is recognizing that we have choices to make and purposely deciding to act in certain ways. Training ourselves to become aware of events, whilst they are happening, or immediately after something has occurred, and before we offer a response requires 'training'. Meta-cognition can be used as a vehicle to focus on effective aspects of practice as well as focusing on incidents where, with hindsight, we might choose to act differently.

How do we find out what we want?

Before answering this question I am going to ask another one which is based upon a fantasy.

What would our teaching lives look and feel like if, on a regular basis, we did not do any work beyond 5.00 pm? Of course *on a regular basis* excludes things like parents' consultation evenings, school trips, sporting events, theatre trips, other extra curricular activities and any important preparation for tomorrow's lessons. Just suppose however that if certain tasks have not been completed by 5.00 pm then they either remain uncompleted or we squeeze them into tomorrow's schedule …?

One of the most time-consuming after school tasks is marking. I have written about alternative strategies to try to remove some of the drudgery of marking in *Getting the Buggers to Add Up* (Ollerton 2004). By doing less marking, or marking differently, we can prevent ourselves from carrying home armfuls of exercise books and possibly carrying out one of the more pointless, futile tasks of trying to communicate to students who are not actually there to be communicated with. One History teacher I know never 'allows' her students to *'get past the staples'*. In other words, nobody writes enough to get beyond the half-way page in their exercise book. Although this might sound like an implausible approach, this tactic certainly reduces the amount of out-of-school marking the teacher does. Instead she can devote time to planning more interesting lessons. Causing students to do less of the kind of output that requires immediate marking focuses the teacher's mind on finding work that does not require marking – for example drama strategies, active learning approaches, students giving presentations, etc. There may of course be some tasks, of a vocational or an educational nature, we *choose* to do after work. However, this is very different from carrying out those tasks we feel we *have* to do. Some teachers do vocational courses, for personal interest or study, say, for a Masters degree for academic reasons.

Reflection as a tool for professional development

Reflecting upon aspects of our practice may appear an unaffordable luxury in terms of teachers' busy lives. However, there are undoubtedly massive benefits to be gained from reflecting upon and occasionally writing about lessons and more general issues. In my own experience, writing about certain lessons has helped reveal a great deal about my teaching; especially about the values and principles that underpin my teaching and how these are manifested in my teaching. In short, reflective practice digs deeper into why certain events unfolded and what the teaching principles were that influenced the outcomes.

Reflective practice, therefore, is:

♦ a process of becoming explicit about implicit actions;

♦ a way of making sense of classroom experiences;

♦ an approach to analysing and rationalizing why we teach the way we teach.

Here is an example from my practice that occurred many years ago. It concerns a new student Joe (not his real name) entering my Y10 class. I was told he had attended several schools in a neighbouring town and each time he had been permanently excluded. I was also informed that Joe was awaiting a court appearance on a charge of Actual Bodily Harm. Given these circumstances I accepted Joe into my Y10 class with some trepidation. My written reflection from a lesson three weeks after admitting Joe into my classroom reads:

> It is interesting to note how the relationship between Joe and myself has developed over the past three weeks and how his presence in the room has, in particular, impacted upon Simon, a less-motivated student who I have had occasional difficulties with over the past two years. Today, for example, my interactions with Joe were almost akin to playing out a drama. On the surface, I appeared to treat Joe in a forthright and insistent manner, in turn Joe responded in two significant ways. Firstly he did get some work done and with good grace. Secondly, he appeared to gain some kudos in subtly letting me know he was only doing his work because he chose to and not because I seemingly asserted my authority over him. Of further interest is Simon's response to such events being 'played' out; he is being as quiet as a mouse!

I analysed the anecdote in the following way:

1. My approach of trying to support Joe, to offer him some stability, was based upon a relationship of 'give and take'.

2. I sought out opportunities to offer Joe well-founded praise for any achievement.
3. Including Joe in the class was important.
4. Simon had temporarily modified his behaviour.

One of the aspects of my practice was to teach in non-setted/mixed-ability groups from Y7 to Y11; where all students were expected to attain levels of achievement in keeping with capability and potential. I believe Joe thrived in such conditions because the only expectation placed upon him, from an academic perspective, was based upon his determination rather than expectations created by the set he would previously have been allocated to. Furthermore, because of the wide social mix in the class and the choices all students were given about whom to sit with, Joe was able to make his own choice. It was interesting to note that Joe was able to help others; academically he was clearly a capable student. These are my subjective interpretations yet what is important is this process of analysing Joe's responses and seeking to understand what conditions were supportive of providing a more stable school experience for him.

The reason for Simon's response, again I can only make an assumption, and the following interpretation is obviously subjective, is this: Joe had clearly come to the school with a 'reputation' and, I guess, would have been rated by his peers as one of the 'tougher' individuals. Therefore my ability to include Joe in the class sent a message to Simon; he was no longer the 'most' difficult student in the class and this caused him to modify his behaviour quite substantially.

Creating Positive Classrooms

From this analysis, I can extract some principles that guide my practice:

1. The importance of forming positive relationships.
2. The value of finding foundations to offer praise.
3. Inclusion is intentionally achieved through the mixed-ability organization of classes.
4. Nobody is a lost cause.

Diagrammatically, the process of reflection appears as follows:

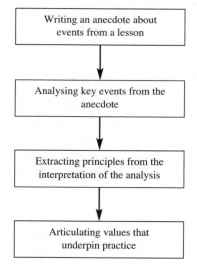

More succinctly:

Figure 1. Process of reflection

My earlier list of principles (on page 26) could, even without the previous anecdote and subsequent analysis, be construed as a 'wish list'.

What reflective practice opens up is the possibility of engaging with professional development from within. Reflecting upon practice is something we can do systematically and autonomously. Of course sharing anecdotes and discussing the analysis with a colleague has the potential to help us engage with issues in even greater depth. When opportunities exist to work reflectively with another person, this can lay the foundations for mutual support and collaborative action. For example, if two people agree upon trying out an agreed lesson plan, each with a class from the same year group, reflective notes about the lessons can be shared and compared. In this way issues arising from the lessons regarding similarities and differences can be discussed and examined. This takes valuable energy, however, professional development is not something that happens by 'osmosis'; professional development requires time and commitment. There are issues here about using departmental meeting time to share expertise and examine practice in a supportive, positive environment.

Conclusion

In this chapter I have explored practice in relation to:

◆ Being aware of what we do well and recognizing desired developments.

Creating Positive Classrooms

- ◆ Recognizing the atmosphere of our classrooms and what the constituent parts are.

- ◆ Determining what we want the culture of our classrooms to look and feel like.

- ◆ How classroom culture is formed and how we seek to support learning.

- ◆ Engaging in meta-cognition as a way of becoming more aware of our practice and of the actions we can choose to take.

- ◆ Reflection as a vehicle for developing practice.

Knowing about one's own practice, or being explicit about implicit values, is an important part of professional development. Recognizing and being aware of our values, and basing these upon existing practice mean strengthening our teaching principles and becoming more confident about why we teach the way we teach. Going through such a process is to know ourselves. It is about becoming more confident and more assured of our strengths and our areas for development. What is important is that through reflective practice, through writing about issues, we can strengthen our pedagogy. In the current education climate of prescription and ready-made lesson plans, developing, deepening and strengthening pedagogy is an essential part of professional autonomy, a key to personal satisfaction and a way of creating positive classroom environments.

2

Values in Action

Standards for the Award of Qualified Teacher Status (1st September 2002)

Professional Values and Practice

Those awarded Qualified Teacher Status must understand and uphold the professional code of the General Teaching Council for England by demonstrating all of the following:

1.1 They have high expectations of all pupils; respect their social, cultural, linguistic, religious and ethnic backgrounds; and are committed to raising their educational achievement.

1.2 They treat pupils consistently, with respect and consideration, and are concerned for their development as learners.

1.3 They demonstrate and promote the positive values, attitudes and behaviour that they expect from their pupils.

The statements above make interesting comparisons to the following quote written almost forty years ago:

> *A school is not merely a teaching shop, it must transmit values and attitudes. It is a community in which children learn to live first and foremost as children and not as future adults ... The school sets out deliberately to devise the right environment for children to allow them to be themselves and to develop in the way and at the pace appropriate to them. It tries to equalise opportunities and to compensate for handicaps. It lays special stress on individual discovery, on first hand experience and on opportunities for creative work. It insists that knowledge does not fall neatly into separate compartments and that work and play are not opposites but complementary. A child brought up in such an atmosphere at all stages of his education has some hope of becoming a balanced and mature adult and of being able to live in, to contribute to, and to look critically at the society of which he forms a part.*
> Plowden Report (DES 1967: paragraph 505)

The fact this quote was written over thirty-five years ago offers a salient reminder of what we can learn from the past and how many 'recent' initiatives, such as cross-curricular learning and creativity were indeed the basis of sound educational thinking several decades ago. There are many important issues raised in the above quote; of greater significance for today's schools and classrooms are the underpinning values that drive policies and determine practice.

This chapter, therefore, is about values in action. In order to seek out the kind of values some teachers take with them into schools and classrooms, I interviewed four teachers whose experience in the classroom ranges from two to thirty years. They teach different age groups and hold different positions in their institutions.

Brenda is a part time teacher in a small primary school of 47 students; the school has two classes and she teaches mixed groups of Y3, Y4, Y5 and Y6 students sometimes altogether.

Anne is an assistant headteacher in an urban comprehensive set between decaying terraced houses, a council estate, with a home-owning residential area close by; the school has 1000 students.

James is a mathematics teacher in a comprehensive with 600 students.

Mike is a headteacher of a rural primary school with 140 students.

How their values become more than platitudes is dependent upon how such values appear in practice. This is the key to separating rhetoric from reality or from talking about something to actually doing it!

The values we take with us into the classroom have a significant impact upon how we teach, upon our expectations of students and, in turn, upon how students respond. For example, I was interested to hear of one secondary school (not one of the interviewees' schools) where the first task for the new intake of Y7 students was to copy the school rules into an exercise book. The decision to make this the first task for the new students was driven by certain values. Whose values and what the decision making process was that culminated in this action is an important consideration. If writing out the school rules is seen as an important task then it is worth considering what values underpin such a task and what the potential impact upon students are. Some adults would see this as an important starting point, providing new students with a sense of belonging to the new school environment; for students to know exactly what the rules are and what is expected of them. Others may see such an approach in a less positive light. For keen, motivated students who would wish to keep within sensible parameters anyway, writing out the school rules may be viewed as a demotivating and slightly demeaning task. Other students may, in their second week in the school, decide to break the very rules they were told to copy out on day one!

However, there are always differing perspectives. If trust, responsibility and ownership are qualities to be valued and encouraged then one alternative to telling new students what the rules are could be to discuss them. Students, might for instance, be encouraged to engage in a debate about what they would think might be sensible and fair rules. Perhaps representatives from each form could take their agreed class rules to a school council meeting where rules could be discussed, agreed and ratified. This is about valuing ownership and recognizing the value of negotiation. Such a process would, of course, take time and energy.

Wanting students to develop responsible, positive attitudes means creating contexts and offering experiences where students are able to act responsibly within a positive and encouraging ethos. To encourage students to think for themselves means providing 'real' tasks where thinking about and producing rationale arguments are intrinsic features.

The following anecdote from James' practice offers a sharp contrast. James teaches mathematics and his first task with his new Y7 class is to play a name-learning game. This involves constant repetition, where each student says the names of preceding people and finally their own ... *I am Emma. This is Emma and I am Bill ... This is Emma and Bill and I am Jo*, etc. James is the last to say all the names. However, because he knows the difficulty he has with this kind of memory task he makes no attempt to hide this fact and will stutter and make mistakes. This brings fun and laughter to students' first experience of mathematics in his classroom. However, James also has a more mathematical purpose to his 'madness'. This is to use the game to pose a problem – how many names have been said in total? Not only is James finding an excellent way of introducing new students to each other, he is simultaneously causing them to work on some mathematics – summing the sequence 1, 2, 3, 4, 5 ... 28, 29. James is, therefore, 'living out' his values, that learning should be challenging, intriguing and fun.

The values we espouse are reflected in the actions we take, and our actions have implications for the ways we want students to operate, learn and develop. This chapter, therefore, is about values and how they are manifested by actions, through planning, during interactions with students and through the systems schools create that impact upon students' lives.

Choice and the importance of 'letting go'

Choice is an important value for Brenda. She believes firmly that children should have the freedom to decide whom they work with. As she teaches a mixed age range and a widely mixed attaining group, she had to find which strategies extend some students yet also support others. Here she describes how this happens in quite 'obvious' ways:

Brenda: *'If I say: "Go and find a friend to work with", then they will ... they are quite used to that – that's how it works.'*

Me: *'I am interested in the word "works" here – do you mean it works for the kids?'*

Brenda: *'Definitely – yes, I think the younger ones are led by the older ones and the older ones get a lot out of looking after the younger ones – definitely ... and I know you're going to ask me how I stretch the "top" kids but it happens – it just does. You've got to let them try for themselves really ... there is a point to step in and say: "Can you do this better or can you try a different approach?", but let them try it for themselves first.'*

To help students become effective learners Brenda plays on childrens' innate ability to help each other and enjoy doing so. Through experience, Brenda is confident that children are keen to try things out; that they will arrive at the understanding that learning is not just about 'right' or 'wrong' answers. She also describes the importance of being able to 'let go'; knowing *her* ability to let go, as a teacher, is dependent upon the strength of her subject knowledge.

This notion of 'letting go' was something I also worked on as a Head of Mathematics with colleagues. In order for students to work ideas out for themselves, to consider how to tackle a problem and to think about what the parameters are when solving a problem, it was crucial that as the teacher I stopped 'direct teaching' and found other ways of encouraging, observing and celebrating learning. Letting go in planned and deliberate ways means putting values into action and turning platitudes into actualities. To illustrate this I recently ran a session with a PGCE Mathematics group entitled: '*Issues in mathematics teaching*'. The day before the session I asked the group to consider the question: '*What mathematics could you get out of a strip of paper?*'

My intention was that through the mathematics they would access a range of issues and principles; one of which was about the students bringing ideas and expertise as well as me offering some. The outcome of the session was amazing.

The first idea one student described was based upon the following array of strips:

1	1	1	1	1	1	1	1

2	2	2	2

4	4

8

Initially someone said 'fractions'. However, this task was not about fractions but about dividing the number eight in different ways. I had not thought about using strips of paper before to illustrate divisors of numbers. Even better were the discussions which ensued about classifying divisors with different numbers according to how many different strips existed for each number. I asked questions about how many strips some prime numbers such as seven, eleven, nineteen would have and this brought out the property of every prime number having exactly two strips. Then I reversed the question and asked for some numbers with exactly three strips – this produced certain square numbers, four, nine, twenty-five, forty-nine, etc. This led to us discussing why only certain square numbers had exactly three strips and it was quickly noticed these were the squares of prime numbers … and so the questions and the problems flowed nicely.

Because I had not seen this particular task before and would not have thought about using strips to illustrate divisors of numbers I had learnt a new idea. However, had I 'taught' the students all I knew about the mathematics that (I think) can be gained from strips of paper I would have limited the possibility of them creating ideas and simultaneously teaching me something. By *letting go* students were enabled to experience first-hand the outcome of a powerful teaching strategy; they also learnt far more and in greater depth. *Letting go*, therefore, in a purposeful, planned way is a strategy that can create enormous possibilities for all learners of all ages.

Teaching in cross-curricular ways

Recent encouragement by the DfES to teach in cross-curricular ways is something Brenda has wholeheartedly embraced. This is because such initiatives closely match the beliefs she has about the holistic way learning occurs. She says, '*Children don't fit into slots and subjects don't either ... it's reverted to how I first started teaching. There's more structure to it but it's gone back to the "olden days" when you had a topic and we joined everything in to go with it.*'

Teaching topics where history, geography, design and technology, and art, as well as literacy skills and sometimes mathematics come together is, for Brenda, a desirable and achievable challenge. Her beliefs and consequential values mean she is able to teach in ways that make sense to her and which she wants students to make sense of. '*You realise that children don't fit into precise slots. What they can offer in one area, they may be lacking in another. But if you're asking for a rounded person, which is what we are really, you've got to go down the road of letting them do what they are good at and making the best of what they can't manage. Everybody has something to offer.'*

Brenda's values of encouraging freedom of choice, of letting go, of students trying things out for themselves, co-operating and helping each other as well as working, at times, in cross-curricular ways impact significantly upon the learning environment. How Brenda puts such values into action are clearly manifested by the fact that in her classroom there are children as young as seven and as 'old' as eleven. Catering for such a wide age and attainment range does not occur by happenstance or good luck. Ensuring each child can develop commensurate with their potential requires a range of strategies to be utilized. These strategies are built upon a value system of trust, interconnectedness and communality which in turn are in keeping with the school motto, 'Learning together'. Brenda says, *'We're all still learning … that's where we're at really. I still get a buzz out of it.'*

Brenda's statement, *'everybody has something to offer'*, is echoed by James when he describes one of his core values in terms of *'everybody can basically do mathematics … everybody can have a go and achieve some kind of level. Everyone cannot get to the same end-point but I believe they should all have a chance of attempting everything.'* Again, this may read as a platitude, so how James gives credence to such a statement is important.

Some of the ways he attempts to achieve this are:

- Offering students a range of ways of carrying out a skill (for example, multiplying large numbers together).

- Posing group tasks where students have a responsibility to ensure everyone in each group carries out certain tasks to a minimum level of achievement.

- Expecting students to take responsibility by providing tasks where everyone can work to a self-determined level of cognition.

- Encouraging students to make posters and give presentations to their peers (for example, what they have understood about connections between fractions, decimals and percentages or how they solve equations or how to use a graphical calculator).

James' underpinning value, of students' working socially, is put into action by organizing group work and encouraging discussion. By creating a classroom ethos of mutual support, students work on mathematics in social contexts. However, the very nature of students helping and supporting one another means they are also developing important individual, personal skills. Because James encourages students to develop problems in mathematics as far as they can he also, therefore, encourages individuality. Whether James organizes group or individual work, much depends upon the nature and the quality of the tasks he provides.

Creating Positive Classrooms

How James manages his classroom, how he responds to individuals and, noticeably, how he enthuses about the 'beauty' of mathematics is something he is keen to continue to develop.

The beauty in learning

Recognizing the innate beauty in learning and finding ways of transmitting such beauty to students is not easy. Although I use an example from one mathematics teacher's experience, it is important for beauty to be recognized in all areas of the curriculum. It is, however, a challenge to consider how this might be achieved. James is unequivocal about both the importance of the message and of the enthusiasm with which he transmits the beauty of mathematics to students. The following quote from Arthur Cayley sums up James' attitude: *'As in art, so for mathematics, beauty can be perceived but not explained.'* James develops his understanding of the quote, saying: *'I appreciate that I can see something mathematically as very beautiful but I can't explain why it's beautiful … if I just allow them to experience as much beauty as I can, they might latch onto a small part of it.'*

James had many ideas about how he could put this value into practice, such as:

♦ Working on tessellation patterns.

♦ Constructing and analysing 3D geometrical models.

♦ Creating a solid called a cuboctahedron which 'explodes' (quietly) when thrown into the air.

- Notions of infinity.
- A sequence of calculations where the answer always ends with the answer 1089.

Strongly linked to James' values relating to the beauty of mathematics is the value of the processes he intends students to engage in, and the perceptions he wishes them to gain about what mathematics lessons should be about. He feels it is vital to encourage a spirit of enquiry particularly relating to why something happens, for example: *'Why negative one multiplied by negative one is equal to positive one.'*

The beauty and the creativity of the process of learning/research is something Sir Paul Nurse (Nobel Prize winner for Medicine in 2001) discussed on Radio 4's *'Desert Island Discs'* about the research he had done into the molecular structure of cancer cells; how they reproduce and how they divide. During the interview he used a painter as a metaphor to describe the importance of both the technical and the creative aspects of scientific discovery:

A painter has to be technically skilled to apply the paint on the canvas in the way they want but they also have to have a creative feel for what it is that they are trying to present, how they're going to do it, how they're going to have impact on the observer. Science is very similar …

Beauty and creativity can be features of learning, not just at the cutting edge of scientific discovery

Creating Positive Classrooms

but also in a Y7 classroom, indeed for students of any age. Everything is relative and whilst Sir Paul Nurse sees beauty and creativity in his research, so Y7 students can also be presented with opportunities to see beauty and creativity in their learning. Much depends upon how their teachers set about creating the environment where this can happen and the determination a teacher has to try to bring the beauty of learning into classrooms.

Respect, trust, challenge and responsibility

As described earlier Mike is a headteacher of a primary school with 140 students, situated in a 'working village' on the edge of the Lake District National Park. Although this sounds like an ideal working environment the organizational structures described by Mike make interesting reading. It is fascinating to see how schools in different contexts with widely different social and economic pressures still operate according to a set of shared values. Mike cites respect, responsibility and children's safety (both personal and academic) as his central values; he describes children as a *'refreshing tonic'*. I am sure this will strike a cord with many teachers who feel worn down by government initiatives, inspections, tests and all those other things which militate against what seems important.

Mike's belief about respect is based upon a two-way process; for children to respect him, he must demonstrate respect to them. He must prove it. A small example of this is his awareness of odd moments such as stepping aside: *'If we come to a*

42

narrow place, it's the person who gets there first who stands out of the way ... not (always) *the child.'* He relates respect to issues of equality: *'There is no question that we guide and we give direction and we enforce rules around the school but there is always a measure of equality.'* Seeking to demonstrate to students that equality and respect are important values must be done through offering them responsibilities and trusting them to be able to carry out tasks. Examples of this are:

- ◆ Asking a student to record the answer-phone message.
- ◆ Asking students to take messages.
- ◆ Asking students to run errands.
- ◆ Asking students to move equipment around the school.
- ◆ Asking students to welcome expected visitors.
- ◆ Asking older children to help younger children around the school.
- ◆ Asking older children to do a playground duty.

Mike also believes classrooms should be challenging places. This is characterized by students having problems to solve, not just about filling in blanks on a worksheet. Students must feel safe in order to tackle problems; they must have 'permission' to 'fail' and go down 'dead-ends'. To have confidence, to 'step over an edge', they must feel secure enough to take chances. For example, teaching young children how to play Bridge through the English Bridge Union (EBU), which actively supports the development of the game in schools. Headteachers who welcome predominantly retired people into their schools to teach 'MiniBridge' are, therefore, enabling their students to taste the delights of problem-solving in the form of a card game played the world over.

A thread running through each interview is how a school's policies and a school's ethos can either support or undermine teachers' opportunities to live their values and bring them into their classrooms. This is more explicitly developed by Anne who has a senior management role and who recognizes the importance whole school policies have in support of sound teaching and effective learning.

A community of learners, negotiation and entering learning dialogues

Anne states:

> *Basically, children in their classroom have to be a community of learners and if I can't achieve that I'm not a very happy person. It would include making sure that children were prepared to and did work co-operatively ... I would also expect that children would respect each others' styles of working ... being able to work undisturbed for short periods of time, to be able to really concentrate.*

Anne believes such ways of working are supported by whole-school policies that expect students to be taught in mixed gender and mixed race groups; '*... because of the whole-school expectation that this happens, we don't have a battle about it every lesson.*'

A strong principle emerging from the interview with Anne is that while she would not accept any student denigrating another, she is prepared to negotiate about how and when they do their work. Where appropriate she seeks to conduct a negotiation in a humorous way: *'I can cope with statements such as "the dog ate my homework" providing I can negotiate a time for the dog to regurgitate the homework! I can be negotiated with about learning but not just about children opting out.'* Anne sees negotiation as a key principle to help students learn how they might achieve something. She also recognizes it is something she is continuing to develop, believing it to be a skill of benefit to all teachers as a powerful tool for working with adolescents.

Anne is clear in her thinking that helping students develop process skills is a fundamental part of effective learning. She encourages students to learn to apply 'rules', definitions and structures to a variety of contexts, including examination questions. One strategy Anne uses to help students engage in learning dialogues is to organise 'critical friendships' where students' analyse and comment upon each other's work in order to decide what is 'good' about one person's answers or what is credit worthy about a piece of writing. When students see for themselves what another person in the class has written and what is creditable, they are more likely to know how they might make improvements themselves. This critical friend strategy is a way of *'getting children to think for themselves'*.

Creating Positive Classrooms

Anne has high, though realistic expectations of what students can achieve and while she is prepared to accept some children will not know 'the' answer to a question, she believes they will know something about 'it'. Her role is to find ways of coaxing information out of learners then use information offered by different students to move their learning on; in this way she sets out to create learning dialogues. Here again, Anne firmly believes another whole-school policy relating to *no hands-up* lessons, which positively supports the notion of students and teachers engaging in learning dialogues.

'No hands-up' lessons

Students do, of course, raise their hands in lessons, for all kinds of reasons. However, the wonderful thing about this policy is that it encourages teachers to find alternative ways of gaining information from students rather than by asking rhetorical, closed questions, which usually only result in students engaging in a guessing game of '*what is in the teacher's mind?*'

The school 'no hands-up' policy:

1. Encourages wider participation in lessons.
2. Helps create more meaningful dialogue between students and students, and students and teachers.
3. Builds students' self-esteem.
4. Helps teachers develop a wider range of approaches to whole-class teaching.

Typical strategies all teachers are encouraged to become aware of, develop and use are:

- Being patient and waiting for a student to provide some kind of answer.

- Coaxing out answers.

- Not allowing students to interrupt someone else who is speaking but instead to acknowledge further contribution will be taken later in the discussion.

- Gaining a range of contributions before accepting an answer and before moving on.

- Using paired discussion for a brief period of time before asking students to offer contributions. Within this strategy teachers are encouraged to use different pairings over different lessons.

- Trying to match specific questions to students who may be lacking confidence, in order to celebrate the contributions such students subsequently make.

- Using questions to build learning rather than as a check that someone has been listening to the last thing a teacher might have said.

- Encouraging children to think for themselves rather than students providing specific answers which they think the teacher wishes to hear.

In support of this no hands-up policy the school has devoted 'closure days' to offer teachers in-service development on the range of questioning techniques that can be utilized. A specific focus has been on lesson planning, about how to ask more open questions, and planning to raise certain questions in advance.

Connectivity

Another school policy Anne closely aligns to her value system is the connection of curriculum with pastoral roles in the school. She believes that making firm connections between cognitive and the affective learning domains are important in terms of students' development, and helps to create coherence between academic and social structures within the school. The particular policy Anne's school operates is a strong tutor system that culminates in strengthening relationships between tutors and students through target setting and reporting to parents/guardians. The system operates by tutors and students considering what general learning targets individual students would benefit from working on; information is then passed to subject teachers who have an opportunity to add specific curriculum targets. All this information is then collated and disseminated to parents/ guardians during twice-yearly consultation days. During consultation days the timetable is suspended and parents/guardians make twenty-minute appointments to see their child's tutor and discuss progress, targets and action plans.

These two consultation days replace the 'standard' parents' evenings where parents traipse around from subject teacher to subject teacher for a short discussion, usually to hear how wonderful their child is. The reality of such an event is the vast majority of parents who attend are often the ones whose children are generally doing well at school. I have often heard the comment: *'... it's the very parents who need to come to consultation evenings that don't bother.'* Under the tutor system, parental attendance is high and for the small number of parents unable to come on a specific day, tutors make separate arrangements. Under this tutor-centred system academic and social issues are worked on and dealt with and, because a tutor moves up through the school with a group, each tutor amasses a great deal of information on each student.

Support for teachers

Working with adults is often far harder and certainly more complex than teaching children. In her teaching Anne uses a variety of strategies and sees this as an important part of working with adolescents to try to maintain motivation. As a manager, with responsibility for working with adults, Anne believes she has important roles to carry out with regard to protecting staff from the exhaustion which inevitably sets in as a term draws on. To do this she places much faith in school policies that are ultimately child-centred but are in place to support teachers in their day-by-day interactions with students.

It's a very difficult balance ... it's about giving teachers the confidence and space to be relaxed and creative in a very structured and dictated environment. So for example ... we have a seating policy, a no hands-up policy and we've got various other behaviour policies and so on which are very child-centred in my opinion ... and yet within them there's got to be room to break the rules. Unfortunately teachers have become more aware of the rules and less aware of the freedoms.

Anne sees whole-school policies as a basic framework supportive of all staff. For less experienced staff the policies provide a framework upon which they can build their practice. For more inspirational teachers she wants them to use policies in creative ways; to rely upon policies as a basic support mechanism in order to experiment with more interesting and stimulating ways of teaching. This notion of teachers using the schools rules in creative ways is important. When teachers gain a deep understanding of the educational validity of and the pedagogical underpinnings behind a school policy, then they are in a strong position to make positive changes to, or slight adaptations of, a policy. This may well result in some teachers, for very good reasons, not using a school policy in minute detail; this is something Anne believes is important if teachers are to recognize their professionalism, develop wider strategies in classrooms and find more effective ways of working with adolescents.

Two of the most difficult aspects of teaching and something that grinds teachers down more than anything else is low-level disruption and disaffected students. Teaching becomes even more challenging when teachers are faced with a lack of support from:

- A minority of parents, who give little or no credence to education.
- Some parts of the media, when they are critical of schools.
- Governments that use funding to pursue political aims (for example, Specialist status schools).

What supports teachers in their day-to-day teaching and in their relationships with students are:

- Good relationships with the majority of students.
- Good relationships with other staff.
- Managers who place the welfare of staff as a paramount consideration.
- Sufficient resources to do the job.
- A set of well thought out, secure whole-school policies.

Policies must be fashioned not to check up on teachers but to support teacher development. Attention must be paid to thoughtful policies that underpin effective teaching, that are supportive of the development of positive relationships between teachers and students and between teachers and teachers. *'Monitoring is not just about checking up [on teachers], action must be taken that is supportive of teachers; its got to be really supportive. It's about gentling the profession ... One of the difficulties is going to always be the assessment culture until it relaxes its grip a bit so targets become genuine, human understandings of what learning is about ... There shouldn't be children saying I'm a level 4 person ...'.*

The values we take with us into classrooms have a massive impact upon how we teach, upon how students receive our teaching and, therefore, how they engage with learning. Because we implicitly impart values and attitudes it is important to know what these are and, therefore, what drives our practice. This is also important because of the number of 'stakeholders', people and organizations who have a range of opinions about how teachers 'should' teach. After all the vast majority of the adult population has experienced life in school and consequently it appears many feel such experience confers them with expertise! Becoming explicit, therefore, about the values that drive us and recognizing how we bring them into classrooms is an important part of becoming confident about the ways we teach, ways we most effectively support learning, and ways we develop practice.

Conclusion

In summary this chapter was about:

♦ The pleasure of learning.

♦ Teachers gaining the confidence to 'let go'.

♦ The importance of working, where appropriate, in cross-curricular ways.

♦ Recognizing that every student has something to offer.

- Helping reveal to students the 'beauty of learning'.

- Respecting, trusting and challenging students as a way of helping them take responsibility.

- Using negotiation and entering into learning dialogues with students.

- Connecting academic and pastoral aspects of students' development.

- Supporting teachers.

How Brenda, Mike, Anne and James turn their values into realities is dependent upon the actions they take in their classrooms and the manner in which they help children feel cared for and encouraged to have an investment in how they learn. It becomes apparent that whether the school is a 'leafy' suburb or a socially disadvantaged area, whether we are teaching five-year-old or fifteen-year-olds, many of the issues that face us are the same.

Part Two: Key Issues

Creating Positive Classrooms

In the first half of this book I have sought to provide a variety of suggestions to focus attention on issues of constructing positive classroom environments. I suggest that through reflection upon practice and by considering the values we take with us into classrooms we can be in a strong position to determine what we want our classrooms to look, sound and feel like. Strengthening our pedagogy is about clarity of intention and developing clear ideas of how we might achieve our aims. In the second half of the book I turn my attention to three specific issues that teachers are likely to engage with on a regular basis; detention systems, prizes and merit marks, and smoking. Such issues are clearly not the only ones teachers have to engage with. What is important, however, is how such issues are dealt with and what the implications are for adapting teaching approaches to the plethora of other issues we encounter at the chalk face.

3

Detention

Many years ago I did some small-scale research into the detention system at the comprehensive school where I taught. This involved making a tally chart of the names of students who had been written in the school detention book for the previous few months. A school detention was usually given if a student failed to turn up for a house/pastoral detention or a department detention. I am sure it will come as no surprise that the same names appeared time and again. At the time I suggested here was evidence of the detention system not working, arguing that if it did then it would act as a deterrent. However, this was clearly not the case for the group of students whose names occurred with such regularity. Some colleagues offered an alternative perspective, suggesting the system worked as a deterrent for those students whose names did not appear in the detention book! I guess one just cannot argue against such 'logic'. However, it is usually difficult to provide evidence for why something doesn't happen!

My reason for undertaking this research was because the department I taught in had not up to this time operated a departmental detention system although other departments did. There had, however, been calls from some newer members of staff in the department to make a detention system available to use as a disciplinary sanction. Having taught for ten years without recourse to using detention as a deterrent or as a punishment, I was concerned about the creation of a system which, I envisaged, would grow in its usage, and ultimately undermine the professionalism of colleagues and create less positive relationships between staff and students. Up to that point, within the department, we had used alternative ways of negotiating our way through the complexities of teaching and dealing with all kind of adolescents' behaviour.

Sadly the department did institute a detention system which, predictably, grew in its usage and, in my opinion, did not help those teachers who may have benefited from devising a wider range of classroom management strategies. Instead detention became a prop so, for example, some colleagues opted to give detentions as a way of 'gaining' discipline or giving a punishment. However, because the underlying reasons did not disappear I felt such an approach was counter-productive. Though this may sound hard-hitting and unsupportive, the greatest support teachers can offer each other is to share ways of working, discuss strategies for teaching adolescents and managing classrooms, and look for alternative ways of developing skills and practices. The latter are long-term ways of professionally supporting one another to develop practice.

Reasons for giving a detention

Giving a student a detention can, at worst, be a

knee-jerk, short-term response which can undermine the possibility of making sense of students'
behaviour and of searching for other, less con-
frontational ways to resolve difficulties. I expand
issues of developing these strategies later in this
chapter, but first of all I have another anecdote
which revealed to me a further inadequacy of
detention, specifically with regard to individual
responsibility.

During one lesson with my Y11 mathematics
class I struck up a conversation with a student who,
for the purpose of context, could be described as
one of the 'invisible' members of the class and
appeared content to work quietly during lessons. I
felt he was not the strongest of mathematicians,
nor did he ever break a leg to push himself forward.
He was not a troublesome person, neither was he a
particularly friendly student. One reason for
deciding to hold this particular conversation with
him was because I had become concerned at his
seeming inability to complete pieces of coursework
and hand in anything for marking. The conversation
developed along the following lines:

Me: *'You don't appear to have handed in
          any coursework for the past few
          weeks, why is this?'*

Student: *'Because you say you never put
          anyone on detention.'*

Me: *'Sorry... I don't understand. What
          do you mean?'*

Student: *'I haven't done my work because
          you won't put me on detention.'*

Me:	'Let me get this right. Because I won't put you on detention, you don't do your work – right?'
Student:	'Yes.'
Me:	'So, if I threatened to put you on detention, you would do your work?'
Student:	'Yes.'
Me:	'So you mean you need me to threaten to put you on detention in order for you to do your work?'
Student:	'Yes.'

Well, I guess in one sense he was right – my management strategy of him was clearly not working; he seemingly wanted me to chase after him and threaten him with a sanction in order to get him to do his work. On the other hand, of course, this could have been a reason or an excuse to explain why he had not done his work. However, I also had my principles and reasons for not using a detention system and these related to the following:

♦ Fitness for purpose.

♦ Undermining the possibility of creating more positive relationships.

♦ Offering short-term 'solutions' which prevent me from developing wider strategies.

♦ Not wishing to spend my time running a detention.

♦ Whose responsibility is it to do the learning?

While I develop each of these below as separate

issues, they are clearly linked in terms of students' learning and their holistic experience of school.

Fitness for purpose

As a form of discipline, a detention system may well be used for a variety of purposes. The difficulty, however, is knowing whether any of the following warrant a detention in terms of certain student behaviours, such as:

1. Not doing homework.
2. Not having a pen/pencil ... .
3. Shouting out in class.
4. Swearing (at the teacher, at another student, in response to a situation).
5. Coming late to a lesson.
6. Chewing.
7. Leaning back on a chair.
8. Passing a note to someone else.
9. Persistently talking.

At issue is how individual teachers respond to such events and how they subsequently interpret and use a detention system. However, problems can arise if students feel they are being unfairly or unjustly treated. Of course some schools operate an 'Assertive Discipline' policy where every possible misdemeanour is legislated for and students are fully informed of the 'consequences' of certain actions. I have no truck with such systems, believing them to be unrealistic, anti-educational and, over time, untenable with regard to staff *consistently* dealing with the complexities of teaching. The single most important factor regarding managing behaviour is not about consistency, however, it is about the relationships teachers build with individuals. Consistency is a quality which sounds fine in theory, but in practice, is difficult if not impossible to achieve, particularly with regard to teaching, where relationships with other people are fundamental. Everything depends upon context and teaching is a job that frequently requires us to operate in highly emotional and subjective contexts; this is inescapable. As such there are rarely 'easy' answers to working with adolescents. However, there are approaches and ways of being that we can foster and these relate to the relationships we build with individuals.

Undermining the possibility of creating more positive relationships

Within the sanctity of my classroom, I often stated at the beginning of a school year with each new class that I did not give detentions. Unsurprisingly this did not result in bad behaviour, insolence or anarchy. Indeed I found I was able to make such a statement because I was confident in my abilities as a teacher to form good working relationships with groups. I have no wish to suggest, however, that certain students did not cause me considerable challenges, nor would I suggest I never had difficult moments or problematic situations to deal with. How I dealt with difficulties was one way of helping me extend my range of strategies and utilize existing support systems within the school. For the vast majority of students, forming positive relationships was a central focus and this was inevitably connected to the nature of the work I offered my groups.

The diagram below is one I have found extremely valuable in terms of making sense of relationships within classrooms. In the diagram 'T' stands for the teacher, 'K' for knowledge and 'S' for students. The arrows represent relationships. So

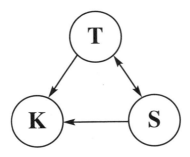

Figure 2. Making sense of relationships (Delaney 2001)

every teacher has a relationship with her/his subject knowledge and likewise each student has a relationship with knowledge from the same discipline. Finally, students and teachers have two-way relationships. The difficulty for the teacher is how they use their relationships with their knowledge and with their students to strengthen students' relationship with the subject knowledge. However, because the teacher does not figure directly in the relationship between students and knowledge, this goes some way to explaining why teaching is such a complex and skilled profession.

Creating Positive Classrooms

Building up sound relationships with students is an alternative to using a detention system; the former is about long-term actions, the latter is about short-term solutions.

Offering short-term 'solutions'

Giving a student a detention might well provide a teacher with a sanction or a face-saving device to show a student who is 'in charge'. This can feel to be particularly important during some kind of difficult transaction. So, for example, if a student has failed to complete a homework task or continually chatters during lessons, giving a detention might be considered a useful sanction. It may be, of course, that giving the detention 'solves' the problem and from then on, the student does complete homework and does not continually chatter in lessons. However, this would be an unrealistic *conversion of Saul*-type of outcome, and in the 'real world' such conversions don't occur quite so readily. The repeated non-handing in of homework or the constant need to chatter are types of issues which need to be dealt with in rather more sophisticated ways. Threatening to give, or giving a student a detention does not deal with the behaviour, it merely indicates certain behaviours are unacceptable. Because the underlying reasons for such behaviour have not been dealt with the detention itself serves little purpose; indeed, the detention might serve to exacerbate a problem.

Not wishing to spend my time running a detention

This may sound rather selfish. However, given the amount of time teaching demands, I really did object to spending my time running a detention, particularly as I did not believe in the value of putting a student on detention and especially as none of the detainees would be there at my behest.

I contrast this perspective with more positive events where I would ask for volunteers to carry out a task over lunchtime, or invite students to attend voluntary 'surgeries' to help them with some work they were doing. Of course during such events there was a completely different atmosphere and I was able to build further positive relationships with those I taught. This is the other side of the coin to the vicious circle (yes, I note my mixing of metaphors here) detentions can create; the better the relationships we build with those we teach, then the better everything becomes. As such we do not need to waste valuable time and energy running detentions.

Whose responsibility is it to do the learning?

This is perhaps the crucial issue and one that is in danger of being undermined through recourse to using a detention system. Creating an ethos where students' recognize what their responsibilities are with regard to their learning is, perhaps, the ultimate reason for the existence of an education system. Of course this is an extremely difficult concept for all students to take on board; however, we know what it feels like to work with a class in a harmonious way, where the majority of students and occasionally all are actively and productively engaging with the work. This may sound to be an idealized description and for some teachers this may well be so. However, seeking positive ways of being, working, and responding are achieved through hard work. Teachers develop skills and practices that are fundamentally based upon students' interest, upon forming positive relationships, and are aimed at students' developing personal responsibilities. At issue here is how we set about creating the circumstances where students take responsibility for their learning.

One way to achieve this is to construct modules of work where students see the relevance of what they are doing, and using resources to help students make sense of the curriculum. Creating a need, a puzzlement, or a purpose to encourage students to engage with a task is a further key aspect of helping them recognize personal responsibility for learning. When such ways of working are in place, then a detention system, which ultimately hangs over all students, wherever they may appear on the responsible-irresponsible continuum, is unnecessary and irrelevant.

Conclusion

In summary, the key points and questions I raised in this chapter relate to:

- The purpose any detention or detention system might serve.

- The importance of forming 'good' working relationships with students, which a detention system might undermine and prove to be counter-productive.

- The value of teachers' developing strategies which make a detention system unnecessary and ultimately obsolete.

- The time and energy involved in running a detention system.

- Finding ways to encourage students to recognize the responsibilities they have for their learning.

Creating positive relationships and finding interesting tasks for students to do, where they invest energies into learning, as opposed to passing round a note, is central to effective teaching. But what, one might ask, is such a big deal if, from time to time, a student does pass a note round the class? How I deal with such an event and turn it into something which does not threaten my status as teacher, where I am able to depersonalize the event and accept it as part of what growing up is all about, is a measure of my own confidence as a teacher. Confidence breeds competence. Likewise the more competent I become, the more confident I am about my teaching approaches and my abilities to form good relationships with students, ultimately to help them form good relationships with learning.

4

Prizes

There's no success like failure and failure's no
success at all.
          Bob Dylan ('Love minus zero/No limit')

In this chapter I consider the issue of how we seek
to motivate students to learn, looking in particular at
the issue of giving rewards, merits and prizes for
'good' work, 'hard' effort and, sometimes, to
promote acceptable behaviour. I begin by attempting
to unravel a quote from Margaret Donaldson about
the complexities involved in giving students prizes
and rewards for the work they do. Later I consider
some implications of teachers giving rewards for
their practice and issues relating to what is in it for
children with regard to their learning.

The traditional way of encouraging children to
want to learn the things that we want to
teach is by giving rewards for success: prizes,
privileges, gold stars. Two grave risks attend
this practice. The first is obvious to common
sense, the second much less so. The obvious
risk is to the children who do not get the
stars, for this is one way of defining them as
failures. The other risk is to all of the children
– 'winners' and 'losers' alike ... if an activity is

> *rewarded by some extrinsic prize or token –
> something quite external to the activity itself
> – then that activity is less likely to be engaged
> in later in a free and voluntary manner when
> the rewards are absent, and it is less likely to
> be enjoyed.* (Donaldson 1978: 115)

Children who are 'good' at: art, basketball,
cooking, drawing … are good at a, b, c, d …
because they are good at a, b, c, d … This being so,
I have always argued the prize for being good at
either a, b, c, d … lies in the pleasure of
achievement, in knowing one has a particular
aptitude for something, and in the pleasure gained
from participating in the activity. A key issue here is
how anyone judges the notion of 'being good at'
something and whether or not other people's
opinions actually matter in terms of the enjoyment
we gain from certain activities. A further issue is
recognizing that if 'success' is defined, then 'failure'
must also be part of the agenda. Of course schools
do not intentionally set about to create systems of
failure, yet systems based upon awarding merit for
success automatically create failure for others; such
a culture is engendered by wider society. The
following is from a *Times Educational Supplement*
editorial:

> *Did they do well or not? Does the first full set
> of test results at key stages 1, 2 and 3
> amount, in the immortal words of one
> puzzled father presented with his child's
> national curriculum results, to 'a bike or a
> bollocking?'* (TES 1996)

Of course it is always nice to be recognized by others for any talents we possess or achievements we make. Being the focus of other people's attention, perhaps being famous for fifteen minutes, standing out in a crowd, knowing someone loves you unconditionally (well maybe just occasionally) are all potentially pleasant forms of recognition. However, we also take pleasure from activities when there is no one else around to acknowledge what we do; by partaking in non-competitive activities. This is the intrinsic reward we gain from the pleasure of engaging in an activity. Having an interest in something and having the opportunity to follow that interest is intrinsically rewarding and gaining some extrinsic reward is unlooked for and irrelevant to the activity. So how does this relate to teaching and learning in school?

Why award merit marks?

At my last school we had a merit mark system. However, I could never get to the bottom of what the criteria were for awarding a merit nor did I ever understand why some students got a merit for producing a really good piece of work whilst others got a merit for 'being good' for a lesson. When students asked me if they could have a merit mark for doing a 'good' piece of work I would carefully explain why I did not give merit marks; usually mentioning they had already gained their prize as an outcome of their achievement. This approach, of not giving merit marks, did not result in students stopping work; they did not 'down tools'. In fact I did not perceive any changes in their behaviour in a negative way. I did occasionally talk with a class about why I did not give out merit marks and students came to understand that in Mr Ollerton's class merit marks were not used as a currency for learning. Discussing this and other issues pertaining to students' learning was all part of what I considered a positive, open and healthy classroom culture.

This approach would have been quite a challenging notion for some students to accept, particularly as the merit system was used by some other teachers. My concern about merit marks relate to reasons behind the existence of such a system and the fairness or otherwise of its usage. Some reasons for designing such a system could be a) for student motivation, and b) to create a currency for learning.

Merit marks and motivation

A merit mark system is often used as a way of motivating children to work hard. If this is the case, students may work hard because they see some kind of reward being given in return. However, I want students to work hard in my classroom because they are sufficiently interested in the work; this creates its own, intrinsic, motivation. Students who come into any classroom are quite capable of working hard without the teacher needing to offer carrots of merit marks to motivate them. The most valuable form of motivation is gained from engaging with a task; the more interesting a task is, then the more likely students are going to want to engage with it. This begs the question of the nature of tasks students are asked to work on and this is a key responsibility for teachers. Finding tasks and presenting them in ways that create an intrinsic motivation has significant implications, therefore, for planning and teaching. To offer tasks which students can gain an interest in and thereby motivation from, underpins teaching. In my subject area of mathematics I use a problem posing/problem solving approach, lots of puzzles and games, intrigues and challenges.

The converse is also worth considering. If student motivation is based upon gaining merit marks, does this mean the tasks they do are only worth or measured by the reward given at the completion of the task? Does this, in turn, suggest something about the nature or the quality of the tasks? At worst, a merit mark system might undermine more 'honourable' reasons for carrying out a task and as such merit marks could, at its most extreme, be viewed as a system of bribes. How many times, for instance, have we become aware that a certain student has been awarded a merit mark because they managed to behave in an acceptable way for the last ten minutes of a lesson!

Merit marks as a currency for learning

Another argument used in favour of a merit mark or reward system is it reflects real life that, as adults, we are rewarded by what we are paid. Of course this is true and I would not deny the motivation that earning money has and the resultant reward of being able to buy the things I want according to what I can afford. However, there is a significant difference between someone getting paid for the work they do, which ultimately serves other people or has some impact upon their country's economy, and the value a merit mark has upon children's lives. A merit mark system clearly does not put cash into students' pockets and the tasks students carry out do not, at this stage of their lives, serve others or create wealth. As a 'currency' merit marks are, therefore, valueless.

But what's in it for me?

I have often found myself looking for volunteers, say during lunchtime, to carry out a task. This might be to move some boxes, rearrange the furniture in a classroom, run an errand, take a message, etc. In my experience I have always found students to be willing and keen to help. Under such circumstances it has never occurred to me to offer some kind of reward ... well nothing beyond my thanks. Students volunteer to do such tasks, but why? It is almost as though they are keen to have some small involvement in a task, to know they are doing someone a good turn, to gain some intrinsic pleasure from helping another person out. In such situations, however, I would not want students to volunteer in the expectation they will get a merit mark; I want them to volunteer because this is how civilized people behave towards one another. This is, therefore, about tapping into one of the most important, natural human conditions; that of helping out another person or other people. Such an emotion lies on a spectrum where, at the opposite end, is the trait of *'what's in it for me?'* This is undeniably a trait within all of us to varying degrees. However, when motivation for doing anything is driven by such a response then we need to look elsewhere for personal contentment.

Prize-giving events

The headteacher at my last school was an understanding man and because he respected my views on not wishing to attend the annual prize-giving ceremony, he always let me stay outside, to organize car parking and act as a security guard for the duration of this annual event. Each year many of the same parents would turn up, glowing with contentment that their offspring had been awarded yet another prize. It was interesting being 'on car park duty' because from time to time some of the students who were not being awarded prizes would come and chat with me. I guess they just wanted someone to talk to. Talking with such students who were not getting a prize was always interesting ... . *'The obvious risk is to the children who do not get the stars, for this is one way of defining them as failures'* (Donaldson 1978: 15).

Such prize-giving can ultimately be exclusive for the majority of students. It is important, therefore, to use ways of celebrating achievement in other formats and alternative celebratory events where all students have opportunities to demonstrate skills, interests, and achievements of any type and magnitude. Closing down a school's timetable for a day in order for students to demonstrate to the wider public their achievements at all levels, in all aspects of a school's activities, would be one alternative to a traditional prize-giving event.

Alternative to a merit mark system

The following is taken from an article in the *Financial Times* (08-10-95) and relates to a school who came top in the 1995 league table:

> *Manchester Girls' School is a non-competitive school. It is not allowed, by its foundation, to give prizes. No cups or books are handed out for academic success or sports. The league tables in which the school came first are a denial of its foundation; 'but since they exist,' says the headteacher ... 'it is pleasing to be at the top. The tables raise aspirations, which is a good thing, but they also foster unhealthy competition; if there are winners there must also be losers.'* (Crowe 1995)

This is powerful evidence that 'success' can be achieved by ways other than offering merit marks or prizes. However, seeking alternatives to awarding merit marks as a way of encouraging students to engage in learning is complex and requires us to question deeper issues. These relate to the quality of the curriculum, the range of teaching strategies and the resources used; each of these contribute to the ethos of a school.

The quality of the curriculum

As I have already commented, making the curriculum sufficiently interesting and fascinating, so students are motivated by the nature of the tasks, is central to developing students' interest in learning. Because human beings are inherently inquisitive, the key to motivating students to want to learn is to present the content of the curriculum in ways that utilize this human condition. Finding out about the most mundane piece of knowledge can be done in a way, through a puzzle, a problem or a challenge, which raises students' antennae. For example, when as children we played *'hunt the thimble'*, the pleasure was in the hunt, in responding to *'cold, warm, hot'*, etc., and in finding the object. The object itself did not necessarily hold any interest.

Of course it is neither feasible nor desirable to make every lesson some kind of entertainment and I develop such issues in *Getting the Buggers to Add Up*. What learners need to experience is the pleasure of the process of learning and to recognize what they are doing has value. The more knowledge learners' gain, through exploration and discovery, the more they can piece that knowledge together; this brings its own intrinsic rewards. With knowledge and the vocabulary to describe and discuss knowledge, lies wisdom and power. So, for instance, Y7 students can gain pleasure from being able to use 'complex' mathematical language, particularly if the vocabulary involved is something recently learnt and describes the kind of concepts they understand older students work with.

Helping students recognize their responsibilities for learning in positive ways, and connecting together knowledge is crucial to motivation. Starting this process of connectivity, of construction of knowledge, of helping learners understand the language associated with knowledge, at the earliest possible age, is vital.

More recent curriculum initiatives such as the development of *Philosophy for Children* and *Thinking Skills* can be major contributors to learning based upon personal responsibility. The more active discussion of puzzles and problems used across the curriculum, the more likely we are to help students gain satisfaction from the solutions they reach, rather than a merit mark dangling carrot-on-a stick-like in front of them.

Using a range of teaching strategies

To utilize students' natural inquisitiveness, to encourage exploration and help them experience the pleasure in discovery, teachers obviously have major roles to play. The styles, the strategies and the resources teachers use are central to supporting learning. Once again, how teachers present ideas for students to work on and what they bring into classrooms in order to gain students' attention are necessary aspects of practice. A seminal text, the *Gamesters' Handbook* by Donna Brandes and Howard Phillips (1979), provides dozens of ideas (140 to be precise) many of which can be adapted for any subject and for any age of students. This book typically uses ideas where students are encouraged to play full, active parts in their learning and as such own and enjoy what they do.

Using strategies to work on students' imaginations is both simple and purposeful. Trying to 'hook' students as a way of starting a lesson, a topic or a module of work is one way of working on their imaginations. Some examples are:

♦ Twenty questions, where students have to work out what you have in your cardboard box;

♦ Guessing games – this lesson is about something beginning with the letter 'R' (which could be Romans, Right-angled triangles, Rivers, Respiration …);

♦ Discussing the range of objects you have previously asked students to bring in from their homes based upon a common theme (for example, different types of tools, different types of calculating or measurement aids, different types of maps of the region).

Conclusion

In this chapter I asked questions about the central purpose of education and questioned practices which offer extrinsic rewards for what students do by comparison to students' gaining intrinsic reward for achievement. I have raised concerns about creating success/failure cultures in classrooms through merit mark systems in relation to:

◆ The reasons for awarding merit marks to students.

◆ Using a system where a merit mark currency is created as reward for achievement in contrast to the reward growing from the intrinsic value students' gain from learning.

◆ Whose responsibility it is for doing the learning and shifting away from a culture based upon *'what's in it for me?'* In particular I have questioned the value of prize giving events that exclude many and celebrate only a subset of achievement.

◆ Alternatives to giving prizes and merit marks, looking in particular at the quality of the curriculum on offer and issues of developing teaching strategies designed to hook into children's natural inquisitiveness.

To complete the chapter, I would like to make reference to a quote from Dewey (1938): *'The most important attitude that can be formed is that of desire to go on learning.'* This captures an important part of the fundamental reason why children go to school to be educated; it connects together the social and the educational. Fostering good attitudes towards learning, based upon the pleasure of learning, is far more valuable than any prize that might be on offer. Helping students develop good attitudes towards learning, to gain pleasure from engaging in the tasks we provide, and the resulting activities they carry out, are ways of shifting the focus away from any prize which may be on offer. The ultimate prize is for students to recognize they are learning for their own benefit. There is no better feeling, as a teacher, to recognize those moments in a classroom when a group of adolescents are beavering away at a task and when the atmosphere in a classroom is one of endeavour, not for the sake of any prize, but because they are sufficiently interested in what they are doing.

5

Smoking

*Almost a quarter of Britain's 15 year-olds –
21% of boys and 26% of girls – are regular
smokers – despite the fact that it is illegal to
sell cigarettes to children aged under 16.*
(www.nosmokingday.org.ok)

Schools generally have a rule relating to no smoking
and in some schools this rule is intended to apply as
equally to staff and visitors, as it is to students. As a
reformed smoker, I recognize my over zealous
reaction to smoking. However, given the information we have about the dangers of smoking, the
acceptance of dire warnings on cigarette packets,
and litigation against and compensation paid by the
tobacco industry, educating our students about the
dangers of smoking is clearly an important aspect of
school. The important issue is how the process of
anti-smoking education is carried out and matching
this against the images and the perceptions of
grown up-ness that smoking carries with it.

As a 'young' teacher it occurred to me that there
was an imbalance of resources of my time and
energy in trying to prevent students from smoking
when a multi-million dollar industry was trying to
get them to do just the opposite. Teachers are
expected to reprimand students who they see

smoking. Yet the moment students go through the school gates there are many inducements through advertising, peer pressure and certain popular role models that strongly encourage youngsters to smoke. Such stimuli or encouragement may not always be explicit or intentional; we often adopt habits and mannerisms implicit within the circles we move and the contexts within which we operate.

I questioned whether I was prepared to put negative energy into students who smoked, particularly as some may have parental acknowledgement of their smoking habit or even be encouraged to smoke. Even successive governments have shown reluctance to take on the tobacco industry. I also considered whether it would make my life, as a teacher, so much 'easier' if I ignored all those students I saw smoking; to save energy for what I saw as the important parts of the job – planning and teaching lessons. However, to take this line seemed to be ducking my responsibilities. I therefore had to decide what I could do and how I might be able to use whatever influence I may have, as a teacher, to engage with students about their smoking habits. Somewhere between the poles of going ballistic and ignoring those who smoke there are actions we can take, to carry out our responsibilities as teachers and be seen to be doing our job 'properly'. Whatever actions we take on this spectrum it is important to maintain a sense of proportion about the magnitude of the misdemeanour. My concern is how a teacher might respond in ways that may have a productive impact;

to engage with issues of smoking from a health-related perspective in contrast to a rule-breaking standpoint.

Whether teachers should be expected to take certain actions or use specific sanctions in response to something that has far wider dimensions than a school issue is in need of consideration. So, for example, putting a student on detention as a punishment for smoking might actually be counterproductive. I have written about using detention systems as a sanction *per se* in Chapter 3. Here I return to the theme of situations within education being seen in black or white, by contrast to recognizing the complexities involved and acknowledging there are no quick fixes; only different ways of responding to events and different ways of resolving situations.

If a student is put on detention because they have transgressed a school rule about smoking, then perhaps it is the school rule that needs to be understood. We cannot put the main perpetuators, the tobacco industry, in detention nor is it likely a school can do much about a shopkeeper who sells cigarettes to youngsters. A school cannot place a parent or a guardian on detention who may not only be aware of their child's smoking habit, but who might endorse it. This begs questions about what can be done and where the main responsibility lies. Schools and teachers are only part of wider society; they are, nevertheless, at the forefront of society's expectations and sometimes, with the blame culture, when naming and shaming grabs the headlines, schools and teachers are placed under unenviable pressure to act and find solutions to incredibly complex issues.

As further disturbing information from the No Smoking Day website suggests, schools and teachers are continually faced with smoking amongst the teenage population:

◆ More than 80% of smokers take up the habit as teenagers;

◆ In the United Kingdom about 450 children start smoking every day.

Any action a school decides to take, in an attempt to kerb youngsters' smoking, needs to be seen as part of a coherent strategy within society as a whole rather than in isolated, separated ways. There are, for example, agencies such as Public Health Development creating *Smoking Cessation* packs intended to offer support to students in schools who have asked for help to break their smoking habit. Smoking cessation initiatives are already operating in some schools in Lancashire and Cumbria. This initiative is seen as a long-term strategy and has implications for the relative value of short-term responses some schools may use. It is important for whole-school policies to be supportive of and actively work towards helping students who smoke to quit. Whole-school policies can also provide a basis of expectation so individual teachers understand what is expected of them in terms of how to deal with smoking-related issues.

While smoking already receives attention through personal, social and health education (PSHE) programmes, this can only be part of a wider set of contributions. Schools can, and many do, take on the responsibility to carry out work on issues of smoking in other areas of the curriculum as well as through PSHE. In this way different perspectives can be offered within different learning contexts and engaged with more frequently. For example:

- In science lessons students can be taught about the health risks of smoking from biological and chemical perspectives.

- In mathematics lessons students can be taught about death rates amongst smokers taking both a statistical perspective and considering the arithmetical/financial cost of smoking (also see below).

- In art lessons students can be encouraged to portray both the anti-social and the health hazards associated with smoking (kissing ashtrays comes to mind).

- In history lessons students can find out about the growth of the tobacco industry in the UK and learn who are the main benefactors.

- In English lessons students could write articles, poems or text messages or create warning posters about the dangers of smoking.

- In P.E. lessons there is an abundance of opportunities to engage students in health-related aspects of smoking such as reduction of lung capacity and respiratory problems, making it more difficult to run and, therefore, to take an active part in many sporting activities.

Creating Positive Classrooms

The key here is about educating students about the dangers of smoking on a wide number of fronts so they can see this is not only an issue dealt with in PSHE. On a more individual basis parents might be informed about students who have been found smoking during the school day; this could essentially be a factual, informative letter rather than a condemnatory one. Such information may not come as a shock to some parents although to others it may serve to raise awareness. However, a school cannot predict how such information might be received or dealt with.

A further possibility is something that would form the basis of students carrying out a joint project in mathematics and English lessons. This would be to carry out some data handling work, perhaps with students in the 14–16 age range. The idea would be to collect anonymous 'truth' data once each year from every student in the school, perhaps close to No Smoking day (which usually falls mid-March). Information might be collected about students' smoking habits, based upon age, gender, the degree of consumption, etc. Below is an example of information that might be collected:

If you smoke, answer the following questions:

1. Age
2. Sex
3. Does/do your parent/parents smoke?
4. What proportion of your immediate family smoke (excluding yourself)?

5. How many of your friends smoke?

6. At what age did you begin smoking?

7. How many cigarettes did you smoke yesterday?

8. How many cigarettes do you smoke in a week?

9. Has your smoking habit increased in the last twelve months?

10. Can you remember under what circumstances you smoked your first cigarette?

11. Try to list the two strongest reasons that caused you to begin smoking.

12. Have you ever thought about or tried to stop smoking?

13. How much money do you think you spend on cigarettes each week?

If you do not smoke, answer these questions:

1. What we your two main reasons for not smoking?

2. Are you ever tempted to smoke?

3. Do your parents smoke?

4. How many of your closest friend smoke?

5. What are your main reasons for not smoking?

6. Do you recognize or feel there are pressures on you to smoke? If so, list some of these.

Gathering such information as truthfully as possible is a key component and hence the need for anonymity. There are also important ethical issues here, about students consenting to provide such information. It is important that the school is not portrayed as acting as a 'snoop'; information is being collected for the general good of students and staff. Collaboration between mathematics and English departments may be considered useful here, so analysis of work done in mathematics might be discussed, written up and presented in English lessons. Comparisons with previous years' findings, such as looking for trends and changes in smoking habits, would create a sense of whether any progress, with regard to reducing smoking, is taking place.

Were such a 'module' of work to appear as a topic in mathematics and English departments' schemes of work, this would provide the basis for valuable cross-curricular activities. Such an initiative would obviously require some joint planning, yet the benefits in terms of students physical health combined with opportunities for curriculum development which focuses on 'real life' information cannot be understated. Analysis and presentation of data is clearly important and pairs of students could produce reports with some of the following audiences in mind:

- The school governors.
- A school assembly.
- Parents.
- Local Education Authority (LEA).
- The local Member of Parliament.
- The Health Education Council.

What is important here is that any work the students do on issues of smoking can be disseminated to 'real' audiences, and will provide motivation because the issues are being worked on in realistic contexts. Furthermore, a report could form the basis of a piece of coursework and, given the difficulties many mathematics departments face in students carrying out data handling type coursework, this would provide a very useful and purposeful context. Gathering such data so students can engage with the health risks would be a positive attempt to raise the profile of this issue; sending such data to the local MP would be an attempt to keep issues of smoking firmly in politicians' in-trays. Of course such actions would take time and energy and eat away at valuable resources. Whether such projects may be considered worth this investment of time and energy is an issue that can be discussed at departmental meetings and on a whole school basis. Were this to happen then individual teachers' emotional health, the energy involved in repri-manding miscreants, the time involved in running a detention system, can all be balanced against the value of such whole-school initiatives.

Conclusion

The main points discussed within this chapter were:

♦ Smoking must be seen as a wider health problem within society, and schools only have a limited sphere of influence.

Creating Positive Classrooms

♦ Keeping students' smoking habits in perspective is important in terms of teachers' time and energies when dealing with incidents related to smoking.

♦ The importance of using educative approaches to help students overcome their smoking habits in contrast to offering punitive sanctions.

♦ The value of bringing into schools outside health-related agencies who can bring other perspectives and different expertise.

♦ Dealing with issues of smoking throughout the curriculum and making use of cross-curricular opportunities.

In Conclusion

Teaching can be a brilliant job. There can be few better work-related feelings than being in a classroom and becoming aware that a lesson is proceeding, not just in an orderly way, but also that we are having all kinds of positive interactions with those we are teaching. It is during moments such as these when we become aware of the insightful, fantastic and sometimes humorous conversations with students that makes everything seem worthwhile. However, teachers also have the unenviable task of being 'exposed' to all manner of pressures from a wide number of stakeholders; sometimes these pressures can have a negative impact upon how we feel not just about the job but ourselves as people. To this end it is important to formulate strategies and mechanisms upon which we can build for ourselves positive approaches to teaching.

Teachers however cannot wait around for society at large to provide the conditions upon which we can develop practice. In order to be recognized as people who do marvellous jobs, given the limitations of resources and the significant and often undermining effects those we teach are exposed to, it is important to find our own ways of developing practice. Using reflection as a mechanism for developing practice is one way to rationalize and to strengthen the ways we teach. Seeking out colleagues who are prepared to share in such a venture is imperative if we are to have a critical friend with whom we can discuss practice and against whom we can have a sounding board to try new ideas out and verbalize intentions and outcomes.

Reflection upon practice is, in turn, the basis upon which we can become more explicit about the values that drive our practice. Again it is important to know what our own values are if we are to make sense of, sometimes see through, and at other times gently subvert or deflect the intentions of other stakeholders whose values might be based upon a very different agenda to one's own. Deciding for example the purpose of a detention system, the usefulness of awarding merit marks and prizes, and how to cope with issues such as smoking will all be dealt with according to the ethos of schools and the values of individual teachers. Recognizing and understanding a school's ethos and becoming explicit about the values that drive teachers' practice within a school are key elements in creating an environment where students them-selves feel valued and can develop as rational human beings.

A further key element in teacher development relates to the curriculum and the opportunities teachers are provided with to develop the curriculum; this is very different from a model where the curriculum is closely defined and where the outcomes are narrowly tested. There currently exist initiatives based upon the development of Thinking Skills (McGuinness, C. *From Thinking Skills to Thinking Classrooms*, Research Brief, 1999, 115, DfES.) More recently the Royal Society has developed an initiative called *Opening Minds: Education for the 21st Century*. This is described on the RSA website (*www.rsa.org.uk*) as a 'pilot study, testing a radical new competence-based curriculum to discover whether a completely new approach offers a better way to educate our children in the 21st century. The findings included better results in English and Science, improved behaviour and more enjoyment for teachers and pupils.'

As I have commented in this book, there are 'stakeholders' who have, or would like to have, an increased influence in what happens in schools and, therefore, in individual teachers' classrooms. The complexity for teachers, particularly those in secondary schools, is teaching adolescents who are going through massive physical and emotional changes and at the same time responding to a plethora of initiatives that are often driven by those who equate raising standards with examination results. Such initiatives are usually produced by people who have little or no idea of what it is like to teach thirty fifteen-year-olds. At worst this creates a tension between schools seeking to educate the whole person whilst operating as examination factories where the 'product' (children's learning) is measured on an economic, value-for-money, model. This in turn has a massive impact upon decision-making processes and teacher autonomy, such an important part of teacher professionalism.

Creating Positive Classrooms

The most effective way of raising standards in ways which not only 'gentles' education, but society at large, is to provide schools and teachers with opportunities and clear, supportive directives to educate the whole child. Teachers need to feel valued for the multi-faceted jobs they do and not measured by focusing on one small aspect of the education they provide, i.e. test results at 4, 7, 11, 14, 16, 18, 22 …. For teachers to feel valued, this will require not only support from parents, colleagues, senior staff and governors but also by government, government quangos and the media. Inspection regimes must be used to support teacher development; notions of humility, integrity and an understanding of the pressure teachers face day by day in their classrooms must be at the forefront of inspectors' perceptions.

To work towards a more inclusive and a more gentle society, barriers to learning must be removed at all levels; responsibility for building such a society must be acknowledged as a matter of some urgency. To this end teachers must be valued and trusted and given the encouragement and the freedom to make choices and to rationalize the ways we believe we can most effectively teach.

Bibliography

Crowe, P. (1995) 'Teach winners – create losers', *Financial Times*, 8 October.

Brandes, D. and Phillips, H. (1979) *Gamesters' Handbook*, London, Hutchinson.

Davies, M. and Edwards, G. (1999) 'Will the curriculum caterpillar ever learn to fly?', *Cambridge Journal of Education*, 29 (1), p. 29.

Delaney, K. (2001) 'Teaching mathematics resourcefully', in Gates (ed.) *Issues in Mathematics Teaching*, London, Routledge/Falmer.

DES, (1967) *Children and their Primary Schools*, The Plowden Report, London, HMSO.

Dewey, J. (1938) *Experience and Education*, London, Collier Macmillan.

Donaldson, M. (1978) *Children's Minds*, London, Flamingo/Fontana Paperbacks.

Dylan, Bob (1967) 'Love minus zero', *Bringing it all back home*, Columbia, Sony Music.

Nurse, P. (2001) Desert Island Discs, BBC Radio 4.

Ollerton, M. (2004) *Getting the Buggers to Add Up*, London, Continuum.

Sotto, E. (1994) *When Teaching Becomes Learning: A Theory and Practice of Teaching*, London, Cassell.

Times Educational Supplement (1996) 'Is it a bike?', 2 February.

TTA (2002) *Standards for the Award of Qualified Teacher Status*, London, TTA.